MY NAME IS LAMOOSH

My Name Is
LaMoosh

Linda Meanus

Oregon State University Press
Corvallis

Oregon State University Press in Corvallis, Oregon, is located within the traditional homelands of the Mary's River or Ampinefu Band of Kalapuya. Following the Willamette Valley Treaty of 1855, Kalapuya people were forcibly removed to reservations in Western Oregon. Today, living descendants of these people are a part of the Confederated Tribes of Grand Ronde Community of Oregon (www.grandronde.org) and the Confederated Tribes of the Siletz Indians (www.ctsi.nsn.us).

Library of Congress Cataloging-in-Publication Data
Names: Meanus, Linda, author.
Title: My name is LaMoosh / Linda Meanus.
Description: Corvallis : Oregon State University Press, 2023.
Identifiers: LCCN 2023003748 | ISBN 9780870712319 (trade
    paperback) | ISBN 9780870712326 (ebook)
Subjects: LCSH: Meanus, Linda—Juvenile literature. | Wyam Indians—
    Biography—Juvenile literature. | Confederated Tribes of the Warm Springs
    Reservation of Oregon—Biography—Juvenile literature. | LCGFT:
    Autobiographies.
Classification: LCC E99.W9 M43 2023 | DDC 305.897/412 [B]—dc23/
    eng/20230201
LC record available at https://lccn.loc.gov/2023003748

♾This paper meets the requirements of ANSI/NISO Z39.48-1992
    (Permanence of Paper).

First published in 2023 by Oregon State University Press
Printed in the United States of America
Second printing 2023

Published in cooperation with Confluence.

Confluence
1109 E 5th Street
Vancouver, WA 98661
www.confluenceproject.org

Oregon State University Press
121 The Valley Library
Corvallis OR 97331-4501
541-737-3166 • fax 541-737-3170
www.osupress.oregonstate.edu

To my grandmother, Flora Thompson

Contents

Introduction

When I was a little girl, someone wrote a book about me. It was called *Linda's Indian Home.* This was way back in 1956. The writer was a friend of my Grandma Flora's named Martha McKeown. She was a teacher. After the book came out, she had my grandma and me go to a lot of schools to sign books. I didn't quite know what to say to the other children about this book about me. I would just write my name and say thank you. And then Grandma would sign it too. Grandma told me, "This book is about you when you were a baby. I wanted the book written so that the people would know about

Linda's Indian Home. In 1956, educator and historian Martha McKeown published a book called *Linda's Indian Home* about Linda and her family, who lived near Celilo Falls. The book was intended to dispel myths about Native Americans and call attention to Columbia River tribes as new hydroelectric dams destroyed centers of fishing like Celilo Falls.

who we are and our way of life." Grandma felt that more of these books should be written. Now all these years later, I'm what my people call an Elder. I don't feel old. I still feel like a little girl. But being an Elder means it's my job to teach young people what I know. Just like Grandma Flora and Martha, I go into schools to talk about my memories of growing up at Celilo Falls along the Columbia River. It was a truly amazing place and I want to tell you all about it. People came there from all over to fish. But now the falls are under water because of a dam.

I'm glad I have the opportunity to teach some of the history of our people. We need people to understand, and that's why we share our stories. We don't want to lose

Terminology. In this book, you will see multiple terms that are used by Native Americans to describe themselves. Like many tribal people, Linda uses the word "Indian" because she grew up saying that. Another way to describe a Native person is by their tribal affiliation. For example, "I'm Warm Springs," "I'm Wasco," or "I'm from Celilo." If you know the name of someone's tribe, it is best to use that first. When referring to the larger community of Native American people, another good term is "Indigenous," which means someone's ancestors are from that specific place. There are Indigenous peoples all over the world, including Canada and South America. The terms "Native American" and "American Indian" are used a lot in the United States. In Canada, you often see the term "First Nations." Terms will continue to evolve over time.

Grandma Flora shared the pictures of the book *Linda's Indian Home* to me when it was first published. She was trying to help me understand. I wasn't really interested. I wanted to go play. Now I'm much older and understand—and I feel like we need to share more stories. I don't think a lot of people know our stories.

our stories. We need to keep them going. If we don't, we could lose a lot of our wisdom. Many of our Elders are leaving us, and they hold a lot of our knowledge about our people. Our future generations, a lot of them don't even know about where they come from because they've already lost their own Elders, their grandmas and grandpas. So, with these stories, with books like the one you're reading now, we can keep our traditions going, our culture too. It's important to get it out there. That's why I wanted to write this book for you.

In this photo, from left to right, Grandpa, Martha McKeown, me, Catherine Cushinway, and Ida Thompson were at a Multnomah County Central Library event promoting *Linda's Indian Home*.

Meeting a Little Girl

When I go into schools, I teach kids about the Columbia River and the traditions of my people. I like to talk about our First Foods and how healthy they are. I say to the children, "My people have always been here. We've never left. And we'll always be here."

One day, I was at this little museum in Hood River, Oregon. There were four different classes altogether.

Columbia River. The Columbia River stretches twelve hundred miles from British Columbia in Canada through the American states of Washington and Oregon, ending at the Pacific Ocean. It is the fourth largest river in the United States, with tributaries that extend across an area the size of France. American sea captain Robert Gray named the river after his ship, the Columbia Rediviva. The river is called Nch'i-Wàna in Ichishkíin or "The Big River" in English. Many other Indigenous languages of the region have a different word but a similar translation.

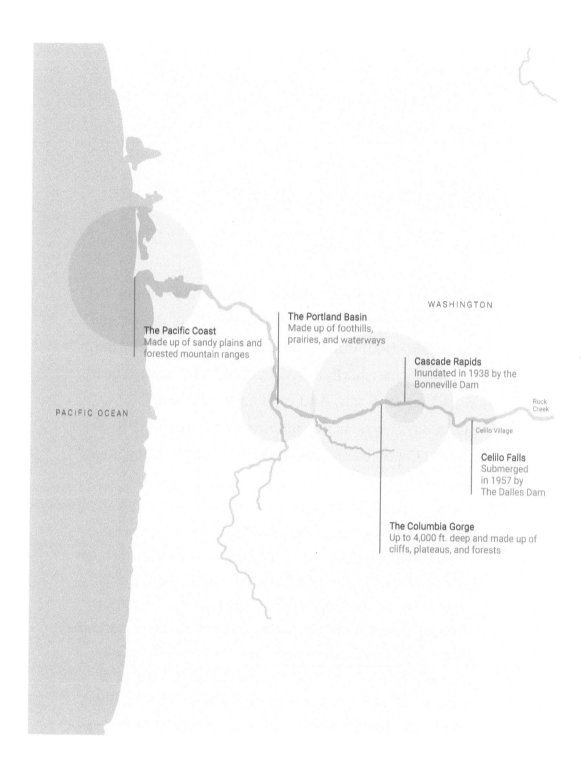

PACIFIC OCEAN

WASHINGTON

The Pacific Coast
Made up of sandy plains and
forested mountain ranges

The Portland Basin
Made up of foothills,
prairies, and waterways

Cascade Rapids
Inundated in 1938 by the
Bonneville Dam

Rock
Creek

Celilo Village

Celilo Falls
Submerged
in 1957 by
The Dalles Dam

The Columbia Gorge
Up to 4,000 ft. deep and made up of
cliffs, plateaus, and forests

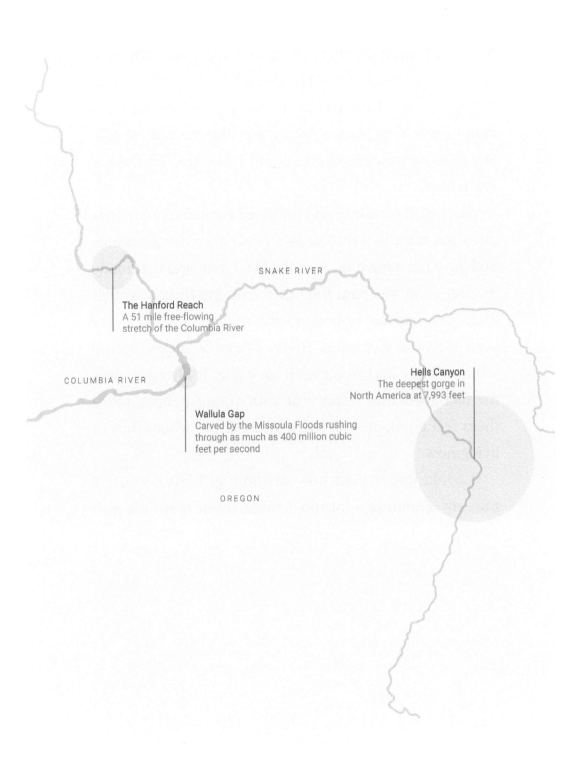

The Hanford Reach
A 51 mile free-flowing
stretch of the Columbia River

SNAKE RIVER

COLUMBIA RIVER

Hells Canyon
The deepest gorge in
North America at 7,993 feet

Wallula Gap
Carved by the Missoula Floods rushing
through as much as 400 million cubic
feet per second

OREGON

Map of the Columbia River and systems.

A lot of children. Some of them were from migrant farm families who lived in the Hood River Valley. After I told my stories, one little girl came up and told me that she didn't know that Native Americans like me still existed. She thought we were all gone. And I thought, *Wow, this is interesting!*

She asked for a hug and told me I reminded her of her grandma back in Mexico. She never met her grandma. So I gave her a big hug. And she liked that, and that made me feel good too. And the other amazing thing was that these kids had never been to the river. They had never even seen the Columbia River. They had never seen a salmon. They had never seen an eagle. It always makes me feel good that I can visit with young people, make them feel good, and let them know about where they're living now.

I could understand how the little girl felt because I miss my grandma a lot too. I think about that little girl,

Map showing my parents' villages.

wonder how she's doing now because her family is trying to make a living, coming here from Mexico. Their life might be hard because they may not be US citizens. History is crazy. Native Americans were not considered US citizens until 1924. And here we were always on this land. There are a lot of stories I could tell you.

Citizenship. The United States government did not allow all Indigenous peoples in the United States to be considered citizens on their own land until 1924 when Congress passed the Indian Citizenship Act. It authorized "the secretary of the Interior to issue certificates of citizenships to Indians."[1] Though the act technically granted the right to vote, states and local officials continued to stop Indigenous people from voting through fraud and violence. Some states simply refused to abide by the Indian Citizenship Act.

My Family

My dad was from a place called Rock Creek, on the Washington side of the Columbia River as it flows through the Columbia Plateau. His name was Levi George. He was tribal chief for the Rock Creek people. My mother was from Celilo Village, on the Oregon side of the Columbia River. Celilo is also called Wyam, which is a word in our Native language. My mother, Josepha Meanus, was raised on the Warm Springs Indian Reservation, which is south of the Columbia River, by her Aunt Flora, who is my

This is a picture of my mom when she first went to Chemawa Boarding School. She's on the right.

Grandma Flora. My mother and father met when they were both students at Chemawa Indian School, a government boarding school in Salem, Oregon, in the Willamette Valley. That's where I was made. I'm a Chemawa baby.

When they were at Chemawa, my mom and dad would take off and go talk in the apple orchard. They would go talk in our language. The teachers at Chemawa told them they couldn't speak the way our ancestors did anymore. They had to speak English instead. That's why they had to go to the apple orchard to speak the language. Dad was Yakama. Mom was from Warm Springs. But it was the same language, just a little different dialect.

Native American boarding schools. The federal government established Native American boarding schools in the 1880s as part of a larger effort to assimilate Indigenous peoples into mainstream American society. Assimilate means when people are made to act like a dominant group. Native children were often forcibly removed from their homes, had their hair cut, and had their names changed to sound more English. Children were forbidden from speaking their Native languages and practicing other customs. As the federal government shifted more toward self-determination, many boarding schools closed. Others, like Chemawa, where Linda's parents met, are still in operation but now support Native cultural practices and employ Native teachers.

Dad would leave school to go fishing and hunting. What he caught would be used in traditional ceremonies. These were very important in our families. And then Mom would take off from school to go root digging and berry picking, the way our people have done for thousands of years. But then people from the school would go after my mom and dad and bring them back. They didn't want to go back to school so far away from home. My mom and dad didn't finish school; I'm the first one in

That's my dad, Levi George, on the far right. His nickname was "Doggy." On his left is Buster George, his older brother, and on the far left is my uncle, Wilfred Yallup. My dad always said to be who you are and learn as much as you can. Teach as much as you can of what you learned. And he said to me, "You'll always be a teacher like your grandma." And I thought, *Oh*.

my family to graduate high school. My mom was in high school when she had me, and Chemawa didn't want my mom to come back after that.

My Grandma Flora raised me as her own. My grandma took me away from my mother because my mother was so young, just sixteen years old. In our culture and our way of life, women are the backbone of the community. Since I was the oldest daughter, Grandma had the right to take me away from my mom so that she could teach me about the language, about beadwork.

In our culture, when a mother has her first-born girl, the grandparents are responsible for teaching her about life, our culture, and our language. When I was a baby, my grandparents used to sing songs to me. They used to tell me stories and talk to me in our language, Ichishkíin Sahaptin—the way you say it is "ee-sha-SHKEEN sa-HAP-tin." I think Grandma wanted me to be a version of her.

Ichishkíin. Ichishkíin [pronounced "ee-sha-SHKEEN"] is spoken by tribes such as the Confederated Tribes of the Warm Springs Reservation, Confederated Tribes of the Umatilla Indian Reservation, and the Yakama Nation. There are multiple dialects of Ichishkíin that have slight differences between them.

This is my mom holding me with my grandparents. On the far left is Grandpa, then me and my mom, Josepha, and Grandma. Three generations together.

Grandma Flora's House—A Very Comfortable Place

Grandma's house was very quiet and very peaceful. She lived in a house that the Army Corps of Engineers had built in Celilo Village. Inside, it was like a long living room. Besides her woodstove, Grandma had two beds on one side and one on the other side, but she would always sleep by the stove because it was warmer. She'd always make her bed on the floor. And I asked, "How come you don't sleep in your bed?" She'd say she'd rather sleep closer to Mother Earth. At the time I understood that it was because she felt safer that way. And I thought it must be hard to get up in the morning! But she just felt it was easier for her to sleep by the fire because she could keep the fire going, and she'd always put cedar on the stove. Cedar smoke smells good, like an air freshener. Sometimes she would burn sweetgrass or sage to purify the air.

Grandpa had a few war bonnets, but this one was always his favorite. This was a new chanunpa, which we call a peace pipe. And that bag was always a special one that he liked. I think Grandma Flora was happy in this photo. They were getting ready for the salmon feast. They are in the house that we lived in at Celilo.

In the back room, there was one big king-size bed and two small ones. That's where my mom and my brothers slept. At Celilo Village, you could always hear the train go by at night. The house had a bathroom and a shower, but it was always cold back there away from the fire. We never really had hot water, so we learned how to shower in cold water. That toughened us up, though. I guess that's what the purpose was.

We did have hot water in the kitchen. Grandma had one of those old-time woodstoves called a Bengal stove. In the kitchen, there was a long table like the one they used in the longhouse. Kids like us sat on benches and Grandma and Grandpa sat on chairs at the end of the table. It had to be a big table because we always had visitors. Unexpected visitors would travel from Yakama or Idaho or from down south. Grandma would always make sure that there was a fire in the stove and coffee or tea. She always had drinks for the guests who stopped in, a hospitable way to greet people. If they were tired, she'd make them go lie down.

Grandma was always sweeping and mopping every day because she'd leave the doors open and the house was on a dirt road. She'd leave the windows open and when cars went by, dust came in. She'd always have a broom and a mop, so it was always clean. Of course, as

Celilo Village. Celilo Village is known as Oregon's oldest town. Archeologists have found evidence that people have lived continuously at this one spot for tens of thousands of years. In the 1940s and 1950s, several hundred people lived in the community and as many as five thousand people would come to fish the adjacent falls. Each April, the community hosted the First Salmon Feast and everyone was invited. The Dalles Dam flooded part of the village in 1957. People still live at Celilo Village today, and they still host an annual salmon ceremony every April.

Here Grandma is putting Grandpa's headdress on him.

kids we had chores to do. We learned to do our chores before we played.

And, of course, she was a believer in the Creator. She had a little altar where she had candles in case there was a death in the community or the family. She'd always light a candle when someone she knew died. She'd have a little bell for when we had services on Sunday. We would drink water before our meal and then give thanks and then have water after our meal to honor the salmon and our First Foods. And then we'd sing a song.

Of course, the cats had to be there. Grandma and her cats! And lots of dogs too. She worked hard to make her home a very comfortable place. I remember it as so peaceful.

Grandpa Tommy and Grandma Flora Together

I miss those days—having a good breakfast with Grandma and Grandpa, all the good things we had. In those days, it was just so simple.

I watch old movies now, and it brings back memories of how life was back in those days, and I wish it would come back. I miss the good old days, I guess you could say.

In the morning, the boys would struggle to make a fire. They'd go outside to cut kindling and bring it in. Sometimes our fire would go out because they didn't put enough paper in with the kindling to keep it burning. My brother's fire kept going out, because our wood was wet since it was raining outside. Grandma and Grandpa would tease him and the other boys and say they were being lazy. And they would tell us all, "If you're lazy with your chores, you're going to end up with a lazy spouse!" Just teasing.

Tommy Thompson. Linda's grandpa, Tommy Thompson, was a headman of the Wyam people and the Salmon Chief at Celilo Village. It is uncertain when he was born, perhaps in 1864. He lived most of his life at Celilo Village and was an avid protector of Native fishing rights. He died in 1959, two years after the completion of The Dalles Dam, which he vowed never to lay eyes upon.

I think about Grandma washing Grandpa's big old overalls. They were his favorites, even with holes in the knees. She'd get mad at him because she'd buy him new ones and he wouldn't wear them; he'd just put his old ones back on. One day she got upset with him and took the old overalls and made moccasins with them. She made a purse out of the pockets. Grandpa was looking around for his overalls and couldn't find them. She'd just smile at him like she couldn't hear him getting mad about his overalls. I almost get teary-eyed just thinking about stuff like that, just memories of Grandma and Grandpa.

Every Thursday we would go into The Dalles to see a movie. Grandpa's favorite actor was Audie Murphy. He didn't like John Wayne, that's for sure. He'd say, "I don't know why John Wayne can kill three Indians with one bullet." That's just the way he talked. We didn't question. We just looked at him and smiled.

Grandma decided to make Grandpa a pink shirt just like Audie Murphy's. Grandma said, "I always got to

I think Grandpa was just being funny in this picture, trying to look like Audie Murphy.

Flora Cushinway Thompson. Linda's grandma, Flora Cushinway Thompson, was born in 1898 on the Warm Springs Reservation, where she and her family were enrolled as tribal members. She attended school at Warm Springs and married three times, the last time in 1943 when she married Tommy Thompson. Along with Chief Thompson and others, she defended tribal fishing rights. She raised several children and grandchildren, including Linda. It was traditionally common among Native people in the Columbia Plateau for relatives to raise children.

make this man happy, got to make him a shirt. Bright pink." She did what she could to make him happy.

Grandpa was very funny. He had his ways of making Grandma smile. He had his way of telling jokes. That's something important that we had, our sense of humor. Even though times could be tough and serious, Grandpa and Grandma still liked to share a good joke now and then. I think that's where I get my sense of humor.

Grandma did a really great job taking care of Grandpa and doing what he wanted to make him happy in his last days, even though she had to put him in a nursing home. She had to take care of me as well. I think she struggled with both of us, working so hard to take care of us.

Both of my grandparents are gone now. I have had to learn to advocate for myself, to take care of myself. I've

I miss her. I was so jealous of her long hair because she used to have it clear down past her knees. That's how mine used to be when I was little. She always has that dignitary look, right? A history in itself.

learned values from my grandma and grandpa, to keep going and do everything with a good heart and good feelings, with a good mind. That's where our Native pride comes in. You know, we're not Hollywood Indians.

Audie Murphy and John Wayne. Audie Murphy (1925–1971) was a highly decorated Army World War Two veteran and actor. He acted in a movie based on his own war experiences and in dozens of Westerns. John Wayne (1907–1979) was much more famous than Murphy. He also starred in Westerns, many of which featured violence against Native Americans.

Celilo Falls and the Power of Water

At Celilo Falls, the energy of the water was really powerful. I could just feel the mist spray my face, even if I stood far away. The falls had a roar that was so loud you could hear it from miles and miles away. Even in the next town over, The Dalles, you could hear it. If you have ever heard Multnomah Falls, it was ten times louder than that. It was an echo that you could feel in your heart. That feeling of the powerful sound feels like the truth of our way of life. I was little, but I could imagine the strength of that water.

And then the smell of the falls, you could smell the salmon, the saltiness of it. It smelled so fresh. There was also the smell of salmon cooking. It was beautiful.

That's the way it was for me. I loved it, even though I had to follow rules called "protocol." I was also not allowed to be down by the river alone because I was so young. Grandpa would get everybody up at 4:30 in the

This shows Celilo Falls in the early twentieth century.

morning. The women would prepare lunch and the men, like my dad and my uncles and Grandpa, would go out on the river with their nets to fish for the day. I would see all of them down there catching fish. The salmon were so big they had to fight to get food. I think it didn't bother the men to be on the scaffolds—those are wooden platforms they built just above the water. I think for them just to get that salmon was a fight in itself. All day long, they would fish.

My grandfather would pray to the river and to the Creator for the salmon to feed the people. Salmon is a gift from the Creator. Salmon provides its body, itself, to us for our nourishment. We need to cherish that. Ev-

I love this picture because one of my grandfathers is in it. You'll notice that they all wore hats, different kinds. Each style shows who they are from what reservation. You could tell where they were from. This one on the far left is from Warm Springs. The one next to him is Yakama.

erything needs water. Our bodies are full of water. He used to get a cup and dip it into the Columbia River and drink it. That's how clean the water used to be. He taught us that if we take care of the river, it takes care of us. We have a relationship with the river, a connection. It's a connection between us and water and Mother Earth. Water has its own intelligence. It flows wherever it wants. It does what it wants. It's like they say: water is life.

I hope you are able to take a trip along the Columbia River. Enjoy our river; enjoy nature and the view. Look at the rocks and the water. There's history there.

Famous Photo of Me

So many pictures were taken of Celilo Falls. But the one that everybody asks me about is this one.

Grandma got me out of school. She told me that we were going to get our pictures taken before The Dalles Dam flooded Celilo Falls. She said, "That dam is going to take our way of life, our salmon, our falls away." She was talking to me in Ichishkíin to see if I remembered how to speak, how to understand. I asked, "Why do they want to take our falls away?" The answer was, "Well, progress, I guess." Grandma was hurt by what we were about to lose. She told me, "We need to have our pictures taken before they take our livelihood away from us."

That's why she had us dress up. Grandpa didn't like putting on his regalia because it was so hot to wear all that buckskin. And that headdress was heavy. But it was very important to her that we take this picture.

A dog followed us down to the river. Maybe it belonged to one of the fishermen. I thought it needed to be fed or petted. I wanted to hold that dog and have the picture taken with it. Grandma gave me a stern look. The dog's paws were all wet from the river. She didn't want my dress to get dirty. She said, "We have enough dogs at the house; you don't need a new one." I think that was why she was looking at me in the picture. Can you see that? She said, "No, it's not our dog." So, I started to pout. And in the picture my fingers are in my mouth be-

This is the famous photo of me that you see around a lot.

cause I wanted to cry. I really wanted that dog but looking back now, I see it was something I needed to learn,
that I don't take somebody else's things without asking.

This is a version that shows the dog I wanted to pet.

Trading Gives More to People Than Money

We never really had money. We traded and bartered with what we had. That's what it was about in those days.

Grandma would travel to the coast to trade with shells called wampum [WOM-pum], abalone [ab-ah-LOW-nee], and dentalium [den-TAY-lee-um] with people on the Grand Ronde reservation. People use them for beadwork.

Tribes from different areas would come to trade at Celilo too. A lot of people from Canada would come down here and trade what they had. People traveled from all over and still do. We still have migratory ways of life.

We traded salmon. People from the Plains traded buffalo or hides for salmon. Coastal people would bring their dentalium shells for salmon. That's what money was to us in those days.

Grandma Flora's Studebaker.

Grandma was always pretty adventurous. If she wanted to do something, she'd do it. I think she liked doing things just to see if she could do them. Sometimes if it seemed it wouldn't work, she would make it work. That's how I would describe her. She was always pretty positive.

When she got her first car, she went to a dealer in The Dalles. She took enough salmon that she traded it for a Studebaker. I thought, *Wow, you traded salmon for a car?* I guess that's how it was back in those days. Grandma was able to talk herself into getting stuff like that. I guess she was a pretty good businesswoman.

Grandma would do things like that at the spur of the moment. Sometimes now I remember what she did and think, *Well, maybe there's some of her in me.*

Trading what we had was more important than money because it lasted longer. You can spend money right away, but the values of bartering you can keep forever and pass down through the generations.

Celilo Falls as trading center. Celilo Falls is sometimes referred to as the "Wall Street of the West" because it was an active trading place. Lewis and Clark called it the "great emporium" because it was the center of a vast trading network that brought people from as far away as the Great Plains and Alaska.

First Kill and
First Roots

When I was little, Grandma would take us out to show us what kinds of roots we were supposed to dig at a certain time, at a certain place. We would go into the valley or up by the mountains or out in the fields. She would show us the different kinds of roots. The first one was wild celery. It tastes just like the celery you can buy at the grocery store, but the stalks are different. Our roots come out in the springtime. When we dig, we only dig as much as we need. We don't get greedy. We save some for the others who want to go out and dig. In early fall, like August or September, we go pick huckleberries, which are like blueberries.

When the boys get their first kill from hunting deer or elk or catch their first salmon, we have a ceremony. You dry the meat or fish, smoke it, can it, and then you have a giveaway. We have dinner and we give the meat or fish to the Elders so that they witness what the boys did. When

This is my uncle Roger Jim Sr. holding a lamprey eel. Celilo Falls is in the background, We'd also get our lamprey eel at Willamette Falls, near Portland.

We can tell this was at Celilo—you can see how big the salmon were that are being processed and filleted. The grandmas in the photo were always 24/7. They never quit till it was done. That's just the way we're supposed to be.

the girls get their first roots or their first berries, we dry them or we can them. Grandma taught us how to store food in cans. When I got my first huckleberries, we put the huckleberries in little jars. We made jam with them as well. We shared what we picked with the Elders. That's to encourage our young people to provide for the Elders.

Today, I wear a basket hat because I'm a berry picker and a root digger. I was gifted a basket hat because I am a berry picker. I'm a root digger, a steward of the land. I represent my ancestors. Grandma was a root digger and a berry picker too. So were my aunt and my mom. When I was little, Grandma and Grandpa and the Elders chose me to carry on this tradition. It is passed down generation to generation. That's why I wear a basket hat. Grandma taught me. Now I teach my grandkids, generation to generation. We need to keep traditions going so we don't lose them all.

Willamette Falls. Willamette Falls is a historic fishing site along the Willamette River in present-day Oregon City, Oregon.

Sacred Foods

When we celebrate our First Foods, we always honor the sacred foods: the salmon, the roots, and the huckleberries. We always give thanks. When we have our salmon feasts, we put tule [TOO-lee] mats on the floor to be close to Mother Earth. Tule are reeds that grow in the river.

In the longhouse, first we pray and then we drink water. Before we drink water, we say "chush," which is pronounced SHOOSH and means "water." We give thanks to our Creator when we drink water, because it's part of who we are and what was given to us. Then we enjoy the foods that the Creator gifted. After we are done eating, we drink water again, then sing a song of thanks. We always enjoy the foods that were given to us. Without them we wouldn't have our people.

A lot of people are curious about why we fish. Well, fish came to us because they knew they needed to nourish the soul, the heart, the body of the people. Salmon

was a gift from the Creator. They have a cycle. They are born and then go out to the ocean. They come back to where they were born to spawn, a reproduction of life. Grandpa always felt that they were a gift from the Creator. We need to cherish them.

These are the lessons I learned from my grandma and grandpa and to this day I still ask my Elders questions about the roots, the plants, and the herbs before I do anything. What's good and what's not good. They know which plants and roots to take and not to take. It's important that we learn about them. You know, I think our world is all topsy-turvy. Some things are destroyed for "progress." But then that "progress" has to be fixed somehow. We grow our plants and roots year after year to heal our people. That's why we think it's important to connect with Mother Nature. And keep balance and connect with Mother Earth before everything is destroyed. If

(left) This is the way people always set out the foods at the longhouse—the way you see on the floor by my grandparents. The foods are on a tule mat. We put a little bit of water in the cups, and then they put out little salmon, little deer meat, little lamprey, and all the roots. Then we say prayers, and sing a song. And before we eat, we drink the water to give thanks for the food that have been provided. And then we enjoy the food—we're supposed to eat in silence, but I think everybody's happy about visiting and talking about family and life and all of that. Then after we're done eating, we drink water again in thanks for the foods that we ate.

people would listen to us and hear us, they could also have the things that we want to keep growing, like the roots and the herbs and the berries, and know the importance of them and how healing they can be.

Canning Fish, Eels, and Other Foods

When we helped Grandma or Mom, we had to learn how to cut salmon. They had to teach us how to filet fish. We had to have it perfect, just right. When they were ready to cook it, we put the fish on sticks around the fire pit. It was hard work but it was something that we had to learn.

To can salmon, you get your jars and put them in big pots and warm the water up, let it boil. You cut the salmon and put it in the jars and add some salt, not too much—and you fill them up with water. Then you put the lids on the jars and cook them for either half an hour, forty-five minutes, or an hour, depending on how big the jars are. You let them sit for a while. It's just like canning fruit or vegetables. It's just a process that we've learned to do. That's what we teach our kids, the importance of food preservation so that in winter, we'll have salmon and roots and berries.

My preserved roots.

I took one of my friends to pick berries and she said, "It's hard work and I don't want to get my hands dirty." I said, "This is what we do. You want to eat the berries, but you have to earn what you eat." She said, "I've never learned how to do this." I said, "Well, maybe it's time you did because your kids want to learn, your grandkids want to learn. It's something you have to do." You have to sacrifice—it's learning. For me, every day I learn something new, and it may be hard work, but if you want something, you have to earn it. These are the teachings that we continue.

Beadwork

When I do my beadwork, it's like doing homework. You have to set out the buckskin, the scissors, the thread, the needle, the wax, and then your beads, and what colors you're going to use. You have to count the beads and the different colors of beads. Beadwork teaches us about patience and teaches focus. It teaches concentration.

The first thing I ever beaded was a necklace. When we got home from school, Grandma would have all of us kids sit down at the table and make string necklaces. The kids were mostly from the neighborhood. Some of their family would travel to work so Grandma would tell them, "Bring the kids over." And we would sit down, and Grandma would bring her beads out.

She'd buy the beadwork from us for a dime or quarter, so we could buy our own penny candy when we went to a movie. She'd give everybody a quarter because she always got quarters from the bank. She would save the quarters. I guess that's where I learned to save all my

Recently, I was just making some moccasins and somebody wanted to buy them. They said, well, the baby needs a new pair, and I'll buy them from you, so I sold them. Because it was an Elder and I couldn't say no to her, because she said it was a birthday gift.

change—emergency fund, rainy day fund. But that was what we did: arts and crafts. A couple of the boys liked to draw. While we were gathered, Grandma would encourage us to learn the language as well.

Grandma taught me that when you're done with a project you pray on it and put your good feelings on it. That way, the person you give it to gets good feelings. You don't put your bad feelings on it because they can feel that.

My beadwork teaches me how to be humble, it teaches me about peace of mind, it teaches me patience, and it teaches me to pray. And it teaches me to balance my feelings.

I'm grateful to my grandma for teaching me about beadwork, about canning and providing for myself. I teach my grandkids about how I grew up and how life is, the way things should be, and how to take care of themselves in the future. I'm just teaching about what our ancestors did.

Why We Dance

Some non-Native people call the place where they worship a church or a temple. Our church, for the river tribes, is a longhouse. It's where we pray. When I was little, Grandma would take us to the longhouse where the men were drumming, and they would sing the songs. We call our religion Washat. It's pronounced WAH-shat and it means seven drums, which is enough for each day of the week or for seven generations. The songs we sing come from the heart, but they are also about Cre-

Powwow. A powwow is the gathering of a tribe, multiple tribes (intertribal), and sometimes even a worldwide gathering of Indigenous peoples. For example, Linda has attended the Warm Springs tribe powwow, but also the Portland State Powwow, which many tribes attend. At a powwow, Indigenous people sing, dance, pray, trade, and visit with friends and family. During powwow season, these can be held as often as every weekend.

This is me at Portland State University's 2018 powwow.

ation. We've always been here; we've always believed in our Creator. We've always believed in the Great Spirit—whom you might call God or Jesus or Allah.

We've always been spiritual people. We are grateful for, pray for, everything that we have. When we are at the longhouse dancing, I don't dance for competition. When I'm out there dancing, I pray for people who need prayer, like the people on the streets, the people in prison, the people in the hospitals, and especially the children.

When we're in the dancing circle, we're praying to Mother Earth. We're praying to the Creator. We're praying for ourselves. We're praying for the people who can't dance. We're praying for the people who are sick. We're praying for a good way of life. We're praying for the future generations. We pray for salmon; we pray for roots. We pray for water, that source that keeps our lives going. We also pray for the losses, like the loss of Celilo Falls. This is what we do. Just like when we do our songs, our ceremony; it's the same thing when we're dancing in that circle. That's why we dance.

Inundation of Celilo Falls

Grandpa didn't like what was going on when the US Army Corps decided to build a dam that would flood Celilo Falls. The government promised to pay all the Indians for the loss of their fishing sites. Grandma would tell us in our Native language, "This is what the government wants us to do. They want this dam." But Grandpa didn't want us to be bought out by the government. You can't put a price on our way of life. In those days, we had a lot of salmon, a lot more than what we have now. That's what Grandpa didn't want to change. He was a very humble man, very set in his ways. So was Grandma. Set in their ways, set in their life.

The Yakama chiefs would come over to our house, and chiefs from Idaho and Warm Springs. They would have their meetings of important leaders to decide what should happen, how they should respond. At these meetings, it was just all the adults and the Elders, no children.

They didn't quite understand why the government wanted to do this, why they wanted to take our way of life. But Grandpa would make sure that he took care of the people. That was his job. He wanted to know how everyone felt and none of them wanted Celilo Falls flooded. He just said, "We've got to think of our children and their future."

They never really talked to us about all the details because we were young. Back in those days, kids weren't allowed in the longhouse unless we were going to help or dance; if not, we stayed home. You know, we would just play outside. When I was really little, my friend Karen and I would watch the grandmas and try to be like them. Karen and I would take the mud pads from the longhouse that they already used, that were dirty, and we'd go out and make our own mud pies. And we'd say, you

The Dalles Dam. The US Army Corps of Engineers built The Dalles Dam in 1957. The dam flooded Celilo Falls, the Long Narrows, other significant Native fishing sites, and a portion of Celilo Village. In total, the village had to move six times due to the dam, railroad, and highway. The Army Corps replaced some of the housing, including Grandma Flora's house, but most of the housing for Celilo was not built until the early 2000s, and some housing still lacks basic amenities such as running water.[2]

The top photo shows how Celilo used to look before The Dalles Dam was built and the bottom photo shows how it looks today after the flooding of the falls.

know, we're ready for the longhouse—we were pretending we were doing our own little ceremony. We wanted to be like our grandmas.

Grandma was hurt by the plans to build a dam but she kept her hurt very hidden. I knew something was going on, but she really didn't want me to feel what she and Grandpa felt. I think that's why Grandma sent me to Catholic school. She wanted me to be educated, learning both worlds. I was young, but still I could sometimes feel that energy, powerful like the energy of the water, but it was about painful feelings. And sometimes it would hurt me. But I learned how to hide it like Grandma did. There was pain and trauma: that was how life was. I think we learned how to hide things very well and just continued on with life and the things we had to do with a smile.

Grandpa called salmon our riches, our way of life. When they finally gave us money for Celilo, it was in the form of a check. Grandpa tore it up. Grandma told him, "Well, if you don't want it, throw it away." He didn't want

Hydroelectric power. When you switch on a light in your home, it may be powered by The Dalles Dam. The power that dams create is called hydroelectricity. In Washington, 66 percent of electricity comes from hydroelectric power.[3] Over 37 percent of electricity in Oregon comes from hydroelectric power.[4]

that money. He just ripped up his check into little pieces. He said, "You can't buy us out." Two years later, he died from a broken heart.

After the flood, Grandma cut my hair. When we lose family members—mother, father, grandmother, grandfather—we cut our hair out of respect. The person we lost touched our hair, combed out our hair. Out of respect, we cut our hair. These teachings we keep, we practice. It's just what we do. Hair grows back. It's just like life growing back.

Grandma Flora Visits Oklahoma

Many years after the flooding of Celilo Falls, I went to high school at Riverside Indian School, a boarding school in Anadarko, Oklahoma. When I was a senior, Grandma surprised me with a visit. Boarding schools were organized by the government through the Bureau of Indian Affairs. They thought local boarding schools were too close to home. Just like my mom and dad, students would go home for ceremonies, or fishing and berry picking season, hunting season and then have a hard time coming back to school. So, officials felt that the students from the Northwest shouldn't go to Chemawa, the boarding school in Oregon, because it was too close to home. There were boarding schools in Oklahoma: Chilocco, Riverside, and Fort Sill. So those of us from Oregon, Idaho, Alaska, and Utah were sent to Oklahoma, and all the students from the Southwestern tribes—

The Bureau of Indian Affairs. The Bureau of Indian Affairs started in 1824. It originally began as part of the United States Department of War, which shaped much of the BIA's early relationship with Native Americans. The BIA was involved in treaty negotiations, laws concerning Native Americans, and boarding schools. Over time, the BIA's role has shifted to one of support rather than assimilation, and today 95 percent of BIA workers are Native American.

Navajo, the Pima, Apaches—were sent to Oregon. They separated us from our homelands to try to assimilate us.

There was a barn not too far from the cottage I lived in, and on the day before our graduation, my friends went there and were talking about what we were going to do next. We were laughing around. Then this guy comes running from one of the cottages and says, "Linda, there's a little old lady sitting in your cottage. She's got long hair, she's got a wing dress on, she's got moccasins, she's got a cane. She's from Warm Springs."

I thought, *Oh my gosh, that's my grandma!* I told my friends I had to go. I asked her, "What are you doing here, Grandma?"

She said, "Well, I came all the way from Portland." She flew on a plane and took a limousine to see me. She was happy. She said, "I just wanted to go see my granddaughter; she's graduating from school."

She didn't tell me she was coming. It was a complete surprise to me. She made me cry. I was so happy to see her. I hadn't seen her for the whole year I had been in Oklahoma. She cried too.

I asked, "What made you come down?"

"Well, you're the first one in our family to graduate from high school." Grandma only made it through sixth grade. Grandpa, he never went to school. He just grew up fishing on the river.

And the amazing thing is she gave every one of my classmates a hundred dollars. I said, "Why are you giving them money? You don't even know them."

She said, "Well, they're like my children too." Because a lot of their parents couldn't afford to make it to their graduations. So she gave them money to go home. Then she took us to an amusement park not far away called Six Flags. She wanted to spend all that money on my friends and me because she was so happy that I graduated. And she became like their grandmother too.

Grandma Flora and me at graduation.

Coming Home

After that, Grandma Flora took me on the train all the way from Oklahoma to California. We stopped off at San Jose and enrolled me in a college. She said to me, "That's where you're going to business school; you're going to be a secretary." It felt a little short and sweet but that's what she decided. She had already talked to the Warm Springs education department about paying for it.

Grandma Flora always felt that education was important. She told me, "I want you to get an education because you're going to be living in a world that you know nothing about, and an education will help you to find your way."

So I went to a six-month course at a business school in San Jose. From there I went back to Oklahoma to a town called Muskogee for more classes in business management. Grandma said, "Wherever you go, I just want you to be happy, so you need to get educated." She figured if I went home I might have a hard time going back to school again, so I kept taking classes.

Flora Cushinway Thompson, 1898 to March 3, 1978.

After I finished school some years later, I came back to Celilo. I thought I should start to share what I have learned. My knowledge, my education—I had been keeping my life pretty private so I could concentrate on school without distractions. My friends and family didn't even know where I was.

That's when I learned my Grandma had passed away. On March 3, 1978. When I got to Celilo, I asked my friends and relatives, "What happened, where's Grandma?" I couldn't find her there. And they got mad at me for not knowing she had died. I said, "Well, I didn't know." Nobody told me, nobody let me know what happened. They said, "Well, where were you?" And I said, "At school." And I felt bad because I didn't know that she had passed away. My mom didn't know where I was and back then, we didn't have cell phones, so it was much harder to reach someone if you didn't have their address.

After that, I just quit going to school for a while and decided to go to work. Several years passed while I tried to figure out what I was doing with my life.

Family Promises and Education

I've told you about my life growing up and Celilo Falls and what I learned from my Grandma and Grandpa. After Grandma died, I built a new life for myself through working in many different jobs. I spent twenty years working in lots of places, but I always wanted to go back to school, like my grandma wanted. In the late 1990s, I started going to community college in Bend for my associate degree and getting credit for working at the Warm Springs tribe. But then my mom was diagnosed with lung cancer, and I quit school to take care of her. She got mad at me when I quit. I said, "Mom, I can always go back to school. I can't replace you." My mom said, "I want you to finish school; make me proud of what you're going to do."

I took care of her until she passed away in February 1999. Then my oldest sister, Dorothy, had ovarian cancer. She wasn't really my sister; she was my first cousin.

But in our Indian way, we don't have words for cousins. So she was like my sister. She died in August of the same year. Both my mom and my sister died in the same year of cancer. After that, I decided to go into treatment for alcohol. I told my boss, "I think I need to go to treatment because I know myself too well." I moved to Portland to go to the Native American Rehabilitation Association of the Northwest. Then I was diagnosed with cancer, third-stage colon cancer. I battled this terrible disease for nine years. I went in and out of hospitals with six surgeries. In and out of nursing homes too. But I survived all of this. I came through a very hard time in my life and faced a choice about what would come next.

In 2010, I decided to sign up for a community college that was close to where I lived. So I finally graduated with my associate degree.

I figured well, I might as well continue, and so I decided to try for a full bachelor's degree. I applied to the University of Washington, Portland State University, and the University of Oregon. I decided the first acceptance letter I got back is where I would go. That letter came from Portland State University and so I went there. When I saw the list of classes, talk about a big culture shock! There were classes on Native American history! I thought, *Are you kidding me? What are they going to teach me?* Especially when some of my teachers weren't Native. But after a while, I thought, *Okay, maybe I need to learn from how they were taught.*

I didn't agree with some of my professors. But I had promised my grandma that I would finish my education for her. My promise to her and to my mom was getting that education. And you know what? I did finally graduate from college with a degree in Indigenous studies.

Here I am with my diploma from Portland State University, with the landscape of the Warm Springs Reservation in the background.

Listening to Elders

I always keep in touch with my Elders because they're important to us. I listen to their wisdom and knowledge.

Grandma would tell me things and I'd have to sit there and listen. If I was playing around or if she knew I wasn't listening, she'd pull my ears. I mean, not really. But she would look at me, give me that look like, "Are you listening?" When Elders talked to us, they would ask, "What did I say?" They would only tell us once what they wanted us to hear because it was important. I think about that. Grandma was telling me this, telling me that. I should have been listening. Now I'm a grandma and I expect my grandkids to listen to me. A lot of them do. I understand now what Grandma Flora was telling me, even though it took a while to get it.

Indian reservations in Oregon and across the country have very high unemployment rates. We are the lowest for income, for jobs, for graduation. At the same time, we have the highest rate of suicides, alcohol abuse, and drug

Grandpa and me.

abuse. So I feel lucky to be here today. If I didn't listen to my grandma and grandpa, I don't know where I would be. With their knowledge and wisdom, I've learned how to live, how to take care of myself, and how to support myself. How to live in both worlds.

My grandma always told me, "Never be afraid." I think Grandma was trying to teach me about a future I wasn't aware of. She was teaching me about life in general, how to be, how to take care, how to prepare for the future. It was a future I didn't like but would have to live through.

Now it's that future. Now I go into schools and teach children about my life and Native knowledge.

When I first started talking about it with the students it hurt me, thinking of the falls. When you miss something so much, you still remember the way it was. But I was happy to share my stories, my pictures, and the book about me. I wanted to say, "Hey, this is who we are." And I'm hoping that someday, people will know more about who we are. It needs to be brought into the schools. That's why I always want students to know the land, the people who live on it, where they're from, and the history of it. That's why I go into schools and read the first *Linda's Indian Home* and show the kids native plants like camas bulbs and talk about fishing. I tell them about my childhood at Celilo.

Sharing my stories reminds me of Grandma. When she was around kids, she felt comfortable; she felt that love. I think sharing my story is important. And I feel like people need to know what it was like for us—how hard it is to live this life sometimes. But we appreciate the life that we have now. I mean, it's a struggle, but hey, we all struggle. We are all survivors.

Grandma always made sure that I had neat hair. You know, sometimes when she didn't have much to say, she'd sing us a song—to get up and dance, just to share what we do. I thought that was important. And I'm glad that she taught me what I'm supposed to do.

While it hurts sometimes, the truth needs to come out, you know. Tell the truth about it. Because the truth does need to come out.

And hopefully, in the future, everybody will get along with and know each other better, and acknowledge the land and the people and our history. And hopefully, we can all share the stories together.

I just feel like that's part of what I want to do: be a grandma to a lot of these kids, like my grandma was to a lot of kids. We need more of that. We need more grandmas to share their stories. That was one of the reasons I felt it was important to share. We're losing what we have. And we don't need to lose it because we have our future generations, and they need to continue what our grandmas are sharing. Our way of life. Our stories. Our history. The love we have for the people. It's important.

Here I am with students at a Confluence in the Classroom program.

My Name is LaMoosh

My Elders taught me to introduce myself first in our Native tongue. We always say our Indian name first and who we are, and then our English name. No matter where I go, even in schools, I try to introduce myself in my Native language. It's a way of being respectful and honoring who you are in your tribe. I see a lot of other tribes that do that too. So I always say, "You can call me Linda, but my Indian name is LaMoosh."

It's important because that was Grandma Flora's Indian name. And after she passed away, and many years later when I was going through my cancer treatment, my Aunt Hilda said, "I think you need to get your Indian name." Because they didn't know whether I was going to beat the cancer or die from it.

In our culture, we need to have an Indian name before we die so that we can get ourselves to the other side. We don't have heaven or hell. We just have the other side. It's just the way our culture is. So, it's always good to have an Indian name. If you hear of people with Indian

I was five years old at this longhouse event.

names, you know why. We teach that it's always good for our young people to have an Indian name that comes from an ancestor who's gone. That way, people would know that name.

That's why it was so special to me that my aunt explained that I should have my Grandma Flora's Indian name because of who she was, an advocate for Indian people and a strong woman, fighting for salmon and our way of life. My aunt told me I was raised by her, and I need to carry on her name by doing what I'm doing. I teach students about growing up at Celilo Falls. I talk to them about traditional foods and how important they are. And I'm glad that I am able to do this. I think it is important to continue what my grandma wanted me to do, carry on our traditions.

You may ask, What does your Indian name mean? How does it translate into English? One time I asked Grandma Flora what it meant, and she told me, "It means a wildflower floating against the river." In my language,

Ichishkíin Sahaptin, it is a longer word, but the short version is LaMoosh. I guess I do have a lot of Grandma in me. I'm a little flower in the Big River.

In this photo, I am at the Warm Springs Powwow in 2015.

Afterword: Our Process

When Linda asked Confluence (Colin Fogarty and Lily Hart) and Dr. Katy Barber to work on a book with her, we were deeply honored. We started by re-reading a transcript of an interview done with Linda in 2012. Then, we began conducting more interview recordings with her. Because of COVID, these were all over Zoom. It was a challenge at first to get used to this strange, less personal format, but we soon proved that we could still engage with each other in this way. This continued for several months—sessions every few weeks where we listened to Linda. Sometimes an event happening in her life or the world prompted something. Sometimes a question from us did, and then that thought and answer led to another story. Things flowed in their own way.

As we listened and recorded, we also transcribed every word. When we finished a fair amount of transcripts, we began to identify, along with Linda, the major themes of her stories. Education. Flora Thompson's legacy. Elders and the next generation. Survival. Our group then identified more specific themes. After Linda approved the list, we began to think about content arrangement. Linda decided that we should all take a try at content arranging—we each took a few themes and arranged content to create a short story based on that theme. Often this took little "arranging" because the whole story was simply there in the transcript. Sometimes the story was told twice, in two different sessions, so we would combine content from each.

We presented drafts to Linda for her approval, a process that included reading them out loud. Once Linda gave her feedback, we began to work on the others, sharing them as we went along.

We have supported Linda in telling her story with these types of editorial suggestions and tried to do so by using a method called "transformational listening," which was used in the recent *As I Remember It* by Elsie Paul. Yet Linda is the sole author of the book. Her voice is on every page of the narrative; she is the speaker, and we have been the listeners.

Lily Hart, Katy Barber, and Colin Fogarty

Lily Hart is the digital manager for Confluence and a PhD student at the University of British Columbia. **Dr. Katy Barber** is the author of *In Defense of Wyam: Native-White Alliances and the Struggle for Celilo Village* (University of Washington Press, 2018). **Colin Fogarty** is the executive director of Confluence.

Acknowledgments

There were many hands in this book. Thanks go to the collaborators on this project—Katrine Barber, Colin Fogarty, and Lily Hart—who all listened to and recorded Linda's words.

Thank you to the wonderful staff at Oregon State University Press, who supported this work in many ways. To Kim Hogeland, for championing this project since the beginning, and to Marty Brown and Micki Reaman. And to the cover designer Ray Rivera. Thank you to the manuscript's peer reviewers, Angie Morrill and Shana Brown, for their helpful suggestions and careful reading. And to Patsy Whitefoot, a Confluence Board Member, for also taking the time to do a thoughtful read-through. And thanks to the Meyer Memorial Trust, whose funding supported work on this project.

Thank you to those who so helpfully provided archival photos. Thank you to Thomas Robinson of the Historic Photo Archive, Anna Goodwin and Arthur Babitiz of the Hood River History Museum, the Oregon Historical Society, Dave Killen of the Oregonian Archives,

Alex Fergus of the Northwest Museum of Arts and Culture Archives, Ruba Sadi of the University of Washington Special Collections and Archives, Jermayne Tuckta of the Warm Springs Museum, and Carlos Pelley Yakima Memory Archives. Thank you also to Carol Craig and Susan Buce for sending historical photos they came across of Celilo and the Thompson family.

So many people supported these book through inspiration, conversation, and existence. To Elizabeth Woody, to Celilo Village, and to Olsen Meanus and Karen Whitford. Thank you to classmates at Portland State. And to the creative team of the theater production *Ghosts of Celilo*, who put their heart into the play provided inspiration that "there should be a book about Celilo."

Thank you to Martha and Archie McKeown. Thank you to Flora and Tommy Thompson. And thank you to everyone who listens.

Thank you to all those people who have listened to my stories and encouraged me to tell them. To the people that listen to me tell the story from the heart, which is how I was always taught. My Grandma Flora always said you're telling the truth when you speak from the heart. You can always write and change everything you write now, but when you talk, you talk from the heart. —Linda Meanus

Discussion Questions for My Name Is LaMoosh

Written by Lily Hart and Heather Gurko. Vetted by Patricia Whitefoot, Yakama educator and member of the Confluence advisory community.

Linda speaks of several different kinds of homes. The home Martha McKewon wrote about, Flora's house, Linda's own home today, and how family makes a home. What do you think makes a home?

What are some of the ways Linda's Grandma Flora protested against The Dalles Dam? What are other ways Flora protested?

What are some of the ways Linda defines her identity? What are some of the ways Grandma Flora defines Columbia River tribal identity?

What are some ways Flora and Tommy created a space for the community?

How are names important to Linda and her community? Why is your name important to you?

Linda says "We're not Hollywood Indians." Do you know what Hollywood Indians are? Have you seen examples?

Linda's parents both went to Chemawa Indian School. Why did the US government send Native American children to boarding school and what type of harm did it do?

Why are Celilo Falls and Celilo Village so important to Linda and her grandparents?

Do you know where Celilo is? Have you ever been there?

Why is listening to Elders so important? What are some examples of Linda learning from her Elders, and how have you learned from Linda?

Do you have Elders in your life? How are they special to you?

What are some examples of Indigenous existence in today's world? How do people maintain traditional ways today?

Timeline
Tribes and US Government Policy

1778: The First US Treaty with a tribal nation is signed with the Lenape Tribe.

1830: Removal Policy. President Andrew Jackson authorizes the Removal Act, which forced Indigenous peoples off their homeland and into reservations. The Trail of Tears, which forced the Cherokee and many other tribes to what is now Oklahoma, is a famous example of a removal policy. However, the policy affected Indigenous peoples across the United States.

1855: Treaty of 1855. On June 25, 1855, the US government signed a treaty with the tribes that would constitute the Confederated Tribes of Warm Springs, where Linda is enrolled. It stated that "the exclusive right of taking fish in the streams running through and bordering said reservation is hereby secured to said Indians; and at all other usual and accustomed stations."

1879: First Residential School. Congress authorizes the creation of the first residential school, the Carlisle Indian

Industrial School in Pennsylvania. The superintendent, Henry Pratt, became famous for his violent assimilation policies that promoted the idea of "Kill the Indian in him and save the man." The US government forcibly removed children from their families and put them in boarding schools.

1887: The Dawes Allotment Act. This act divided reservations into small parcels of land. Lands not allowed to individuals were bought by the United States and sold to settlers for farming. The US government claimed to be doing this for Indigenous peoples' good and promised that if they farmed their parcel for twenty-five years, they would get citizenship. In reality, it was a method to break up tribal governments and take the land.

1924: The Snyder Act finally granted Indigenous peoples full US citizenship, which included voting rights.

1953: Termination Policy. House concurrent resolution 108 (HCR-108) began the US termination policy. The termination act abolished the federal recognition of tribes, including many in Oregon, such as the Grand Ronde. The US government did this in another attempt to "assimilate" Indigenous peoples by getting rid of reservations and forcing them to go to cities for work. Since then, many tribes have organized to regain recognition.

1940s–1970s: Post–WWII Fish Wars and Boldt Decision. Remember how the 1855 treaty said tribes along the Columbia River had to fish at "and at all other usual and accustomed stations?" Despite this, Washington and Oregon arrested Native fishermen for illegally fishing. The Native fishermen responded by staging civil disobedience protests called "fish-ins." After a decade of resistance lawsuits, George Boldt, the Washington State Senior Federal District Judge, held a six-day trial and concluded that federally recognized treaty tribes had the right to 50 percent of the annual catch. This 1974 decision is called *United States v. State of Washington* or the Boldt Decision.

1975: President Nixon signed the Indian Self-Determination and Education Assistance Act. This act overturns the termination policy. It recognizes tribal sovereignty and requires the US government to contract with tribal nations in providing services rather than having total federal oversight. For example, Linda's tribe, the Confederated Tribes of Warm Springs, oversees its own health care systems, although they are granted federal money. This ensures that tribes are maintaining sovereignty by overseeing services such as this.

1978: Indian Child Welfare Act. This law was passed in response to the legacy of the US government removing children from their families. The ICWA states that tribes have sovereignty over the adoption and foster care of tribal children. For example, this means that it is prioritized that a child is adopted within the tribe.

Glossary

Bengal stove. A line of stoves made from 1870–1940. Many old-fashioned stoves you see are Bengal stoves.

Celilo Falls. A waterfall in the Columbia River, now flooded by The Dalles Dam.

Columbia Plateau. A geographic region formed millions of years ago by flows of basalt, it extends from Astoria to Portland to Spokane and to John Day.

Elders. Elders are respected members of a community who have wisdom to share, often older in age but not always. You may notice Elders are capitalized, which is one way we show respect to them.

Muskogee. A town in Oklahoma.

Native American Rehabilitation Association of the Northwest. The mission of NARA NW is to provide education, physical and mental health services, and substance abuse treatment that is culturally appropriate to American Indians, Alaska Natives, and anyone in need.

Portland State University. A university in Portland, Oregon.

Rock Creek. A Yakama Nation village site in Washington state, near Goldendale.

Studebaker. An American car company that went out of business in 1966.

The Dalles. A town in Oregon, near Celilo Falls.

Warm Springs Reservation. Located in north central Oregon, the Warm Springs Reservation is home to the **Warm Springs, Wasco, and Paiute Tribes.**

Washat. A Sahaptin word that translates into "the Seven Drums Religion."

Wyam. A Sahaptin word that translates into "echo of falling water."

Notes

1 *An Act to Authorize the Secretary of the Interior to Issue Certificates of Citizenship to Indians.* Public Law 175. *Statutes at Large 43*, (1924): 253.

2 Diana Fredlund. "The Corps of Engineers and Celilo Falls: Facing the Past, Looking to the Future." *Oregon Historical Quarterly* 108, no. 4 (2007): 688–697. https://www.jstor.org/stable/20615813.

3 Profile Analysis. Washington State Energy Profile Analysis. EIA. https://www.eia.gov/state/analysis.php?sid=WA#:~:text=Natural%20 gas%2C%20nonhydroelectric%20renewable%20resources,total%20 electricity%20generation%20in%202020.

4 Oregon Department of Energy. www.oregon.gov. https://www.oregon.gov/energy/energy-oregon/Pages/Electricity-Mix-in-Oregon.aspx.

Illustration Credits

All photographs are from Linda's personal collection unless noted below.

12: Oregon Historical Society. Library; Org. Lot 1284; Al Monner news negatives. Courtesy the *Oregonian*.

14-15: Map created by Brian Boram for Confluence.

16: Close-up of map, edited by Lily Hart.

20: Relander Collection, Yakima Memory, Yakima Valley Library.

24: Oregon Historical Society. Library; Org. Lot 1284; Al Monner news negatives. Courtesy the *Oregonian*.

29: Relander Collection, Yakima Memory, Yakima Valley Library.

31: Relander Collection, Yakima Memory, Yakima Valley Library.

35: University of Washington Libraries, American Indians of the Pacific Northwest Collection.

38: Northwest Museum of Arts and Culture. Number: L95-66.3.

45: Relander Collection, Yakima Memory, Yakima Valley Library.

48: Relander Collection, Yakima Memory, Yakima Valley Library.

52: Confluence and Linda Meanus. Photo by Lily Hart.

54: Confluence and Linda Meanus. Photo by Lily Hart.

61: Hood River County Museum and US Army Corps of Engineers Northwestern Division.

69: Hood River County Museum.

73: Confluence and Linda Meanus. Photo by Lily Hart.

75: Relander Collection, Yakima Memory, Yakima Valley Library.

77: Associated Press.

78: Confluence. Photo by Michael Peterson.